www.providencebooks.net

Publisher Contact

Email:contact@providencebooks.net

Social media: facebook.com/providencebooks

Acknowledgements

The team at Providence Books would like to thank our friends, family, suppliers and customers for making our vision of creating the highest-quality books a reality. Thanks for purchasing and enjoy the quotes!

This page is intentionally left blank

This page is intentionally left blank

In my school, the brightest boys did math and physics, the less bright did physics and chemistry, and the least bright did biology. I wanted to do math and physics, but my father made me do chemistry because he thought there would be no jobs for mathematicians.

Stephen Hawking

Science is beautiful when it makes simple explanations of phenomena or connections between different observations. Examples include the double helix in biology and the fundamental equations of physics.

Stephen Hawking

Biology is the study of complicated things that have the appearance of having been designed with a purpose.

Richard Dawkins

You can't even begin to understand biology, you can't understand life, unless you understand what it's all there for, how it arose - and that means evolution.

Richard Dawkins

I'm fascinated by the idea that genetics is digital. A gene is a long sequence of coded letters, like computer information. Modern biology is becoming very much a branch of information technology.

Richard Dawkins

Biology is a software process. Our bodies are made up of trillions of cells, each governed by this process. You and I are walking around with outdated software running in our bodies, which evolved in a very different era.

Ray Kurzweil

The kitchen's a laboratory, and everything that happens there has to do with science. It's biology, chemistry, physics. Yes, there's history. Yes, there's artistry. Yes, to all of that. But what happened there, what actually happens to the food is all science.

Alton Brown

Human beings are attracted to novelty: to probe the 'adjacent possible.' We didn't stay in the caves. We didn't stay on the planet, and soon we won't stay within the limitations of our biology. We move forward. We transcend our limits. We go to the moon, and we create the Internet.

Jason Silva

I don't pretend there aren't biological differences, but I don't believe the desire for leadership is hardwired biology, not the desire to win or excel. I believe that it's socialization, that we're socializing our daughters to nurture and our boys to lead.

Sheryl Sandberg

There's biology in everything, even when you're feeling spiritual.

Helen Fisher

I try to show the public that chemistry, biology, physics, astrophysics is life. It is not some separate subject that you have to be pulled into a corner to be taught about.

Neil deGrasse Tyson

It has become part of the accepted wisdom to say that the twentieth century was the century of physics and the twenty-first century will be the century of biology.

Freeman Dyson

Nothing can be more incorrect than the assumption one sometimes meets with, that physics has one method, chemistry another, and biology a third.

Thomas Huxley

I am very comfortable with the idea that we can override biology with free will.

Richard Dawkins

Progressively thinking biologists, both in our country and abroad, saw in Darwinism the only right road to the further development of scientific biology.

Trofim Lysenko

Biology is the science. Evolution is the concept that makes biology unique.

Jared Diamond

You can free yourself from aging by reinterpreting your body and by grasping the link between belief and biology.

Deepak Chopra

In the nearer term, I think various developments in biotechnology and synthetic biology are quite disconcerting. We are gaining the ability to create designer pathogens, and there are these blueprints of various disease organisms that are in the public domain - you can download the gene sequence for smallpox or the 1918 flu virus from the Internet.

Nick Bostrom

Extreme heroism springs from something that no scientific theory can fully explain; it's an illogical impulse that flies in the face of biology, psychology, actuarial statistics, and basic common sense.

Christopher McDougall

It will be the mother of all telescopes, and you can bet it will do for astronomy what genome sequencing is doing for biology. The clumsy, if utilitarian, name of this mirrored monster is Large Synoptic Survey Telescope, or LSST. You can't use it yet, but a peak in the Chilean Andes has been decapitated to provide a level spot for placement.

Seth Shostak

Carl Sagan spoke fluently between biology and geology and astrophysics and physics. If you move fluently across those boundaries, you realize that science is everywhere; science is not something you can step around or sweep under the rug.

Neil deGrasse Tyson

Evolution is the fundamental idea in all of life science - in all of biology.

Bill Nye

A universe with a God would look quite different from a universe without one. A physics, a biology where there is a God is bound to look different. So the most basic claims of religion are scientific. Religion is a scientific theory.

Richard Dawkins

Biology is now bigger than physics, as measured by the size of budgets, by the size of the workforce, or by the output of major discoveries; and biology is likely to remain the biggest part of science through the twenty-first century.

Freeman Dyson

I went to college. I had a double major in biology and physical education, but my major was wrestling.

Dan Gable

Nothing in biology makes sense except in the light of evolution.

Theodosius Dobzhansky

Consciousness, when it's unburdened by the body, is something that's ecstatic; we use the mind to watch the mind, and that's the meta-nature of our consciousness; we know that we know that we know, and that's such a delicious feeling, but when it's unburdened by biology and entropy, it becomes more than delicious: it becomes magical.

Jason Silva

One of the ultimate challenges for biology is to understand the brain's processing of unconscious and conscious perception, emotion, and empathy.

Eric Kandel

On bad days, I think I'd like to be a plastic surgeon who goes to Third World countries and operates on children in villages with airlifts, and then I think, 'Yeah, right, I'm going to go back to undergraduate school and take all the biology I missed and then go to medical school.' No. No.

Tama Janowitz

Biology is the least of what makes someone a mother.

Oprah Winfrey

Darwin's theory of evolution is a framework by which we understand the diversity of life on Earth. But there is no equation sitting there in Darwin's 'Origin of Species' that you apply and say, 'What is this species going to look like in 100 years or 1,000 years?' Biology isn't there yet with that kind of predictive precision.

Neil deGrasse Tyson

Biology has at least 50 more interesting years.

James D. Watson

Men are not allowed to think freely about chemistry and biology: why should they be allowed to think freely about political philosophy?

Auguste Comte

! want to leverage the creativity of researchers across mathematics, statistics, data mining, computer science, biology, medicine, and the public at large.

Tan Le

There's so much I'm interested in that I didn't discover in high school. For 'The Amazing Spider-Man', because Gwen is a scientist, we went to a lab in San Diego, and we were learning about biology. And I'm fascinated! Because I never went to biology class in high school.

Emma Stone

If you look at winners of the Nobel Prize in biology, you'll find a fair smattering of people who don't know how to work a pipette.

Aubrey de Grey

When the first fossils began to be found in eastern Africa, in the late 1950s, I thought, what a wonderful marriage this was, biology and anthropology. I was around 16 years old when I made this particular choice of academic pursuit.

Donald Johanson

Because all of biology is connected, one can often make a breakthrough with an organism that exaggerates a particular phenomenon, and later explore the generality.

Thomas R. Cech

If the relationship of father to son could really be reduced to biology, the whole earth would blaze with the glory of fathers and sons.

James A. Baldwin

Every time I hear a politician mention the word 'stimulus,' my mind flashes back to high school biology class, when I touched battery wires to a dead frog to make it twitch.

Robert Kiyosaki

The human mind evolved to believe in the gods. It did not evolve to believe in biology.

E. O. Wilson

Where there's water on Earth, you find life as we know it. So if you find water somewhere else, it becomes a remarkable draw to look closer to see if life of any kind is there, even if it's bacterial, which would be extraordinary for the field of biology.

Neil deGrasse Tyson

I have never been a fan of science fiction. For me, fiction has to explore the combinatorial possibilities of people interacting under the constraints imposed by our biology and history. When an author is free to suspend the constraints, it's tennis without a net.

Steven Pinker

Survival, in the cool economics of biology, means simply the persistence of one's own genes in the generations to follow.

Lewis Thomas

Some cultural phenomena bear a striking resemblance to the cells of cell biology, actively preserving themselves in their social environments, finding the nutrients they need and fending off the causes of their dissolution.

Daniel Dennett

High school was interesting, because I went from a public school middle school to an academy where the first year we were doing Latin, chemistry, biology. I mean, I was woefully unprepared for the type of study.

Kyle Chandler

We talk about the Internet. That comes from science. Weather forecasting. That comes from science. The main idea in all of biology is evolution. To not teach it to our young people is wrong.

Bill Nye

Art has this ability to allow you to connect back through history in the same way that biology does. I'm always looking for source material.

Jeff Koons

Clearly, enriching the cosmos with heavy elements takes a while. So there's inevitably an interval between the sterile aftermath of the Big Bang and a time when the cosmic chemistry set had enough ingredients to make rocky planets (and squishy biology).

Seth Shostak

Despite tantalizing suggestions of fossilized microbes in meteorites, puzzling and possibly biogenic methane gas in the martian atmosphere, and a long-standing controversy over the Viking lander experiments of nearly 40 years ago, there's still no Exhibit A that points unequivocally to biology in our own back yard.

Seth Shostak

The fact that we can't easily foresee clues that would betray an intelligence a million millennia farther down the road suggests that we're like ants trying to discover humans. Ask yourself: Would ants ever recognize houses, cars, or fire hydrants as the work of advanced biology?

Seth Shostak

Whether conservative or liberal, fundamentalist or agnostic, the more students learn of biology, the more they accept evolution.

Kenneth R. Miller

I believe that all centers that appear in space - whether they originate in biology, in physical forces, in pure geometry, in color - are alike simply in that they all animate space. It is this animated space that has its functional effect upon the world, that determines the way things work, that governs the presence of harmony and life.

Christopher Alexander

In Darwin's time all of biology was a black box: not only the cell, or the eye, or digestion, or immunity, but every biological structure and function because, ultimately, no one could explain how biological processes occurred.

Michael Behe

A permanent base on Mars would have a number of advantages beyond being a bonanza for planetary science and geology. If, as some evidence suggests, exotic micro-organisms have arisen independently of terrestrial life, studying them could revolutionise biology, medicine and biotechnology.

Paul Davies

So we've moved from an era when women's biology was women's destiny to today, which is an era in which men's biology is men's destiny.

Warren Farrell

Natural selection is not gene centrist and nor is biology all about genes; our comprehending minds are a result of our fast evolving culture.

Daniel Dennett

Religion is the best antidote to the individualism of the consumer age. The idea that society can do without it flies in the face of history and, now, evolutionary biology.

Jonathan Sacks

Half a million women die each year around the world in pregnancy. It's not biology that kills them so much as neglect.

Nicholas D. Kristof

Imagine someone holding forth on biology whose only knowledge of the subject is 'The Book of British Birds,' and you have a rough idea of what it feels like to read Richard Dawkins on theology.

Terry Eagleton

You know, I have a lot of books on my iPad, but when I try to read them, I find myself wandering off to play games. Those are books I'm interested in. I can't imagine what would have happened to me in college if my biology class had been on the same computer as 'Words With Friends' and 'Doom.'

Gail Collins

Biology, meaning the science of all life, is a late notion.

Leon Kass

Both in Britain and America, huge publicity has been given to stem cells, particularly embryonic stem cells, and the potential they offer. Of course, the study of stem cells is one of the most exciting areas in biology, but I think it is unlikely that embryonic stem cells are likely to be useful in healthcare for a long time.

Robert Winston

I don't find biology as interesting as politics and humanism. I talk more about existential stuff.

Dana Carvey

Biology is far from understanding exactly how a single cell develops into a baby, but research suggests that human development can ultimately be explained in terms of biochemistry and molecular biology. Most scientists would make a similar statement about evolution.

Kenneth R. Miller

For businesses, biomimicry is about bringing a new discipline - biology - to the design table. It's not to write an environmental impact statement, as most biologists in business do right now.

Janine Benyus

I've always been interested in medicine and was pleased when my brother became a doctor. But after thinking seriously about that field, I realized that what intrigued me was not the science, not the chemistry or biology of medicine, but the narrative - the story of each patient, each illness.

Lois Lowry

No matter how little we think anatomy should matter to one's social and political rights, surely we can't pretend biology doesn't matter in sports. Surely there's a reason we don't let adults play in the t-ball leagues, and a reason most women athletes want their own leagues.

Alice Dreger

Whether it's in an inner-city school or a rural community, I want those students to have a chance to take A.P. biology and A.P. physics and marine biology.

Arne Duncan

I trained initially as a physical chemist, and then, after becoming interested in biology, I went to medical school and learned how to be a physician. So, I'm a physician scientist.

Francis Collins

The biology of mind bridges the sciences - concerned with the natural world - and the humanities - concerned with the meaning of human experience.

Eric Kandel

I'm trying to figure out the biology of dinosaurs and what they were like as living creatures.

Jack Horner

It will be in the convergence of evolutionary biology, developmental biology and cancer biology that the answer to cancer will lie. Nor will this confluence be a one-way street.

Paul Davies

My interests span biology, though sometimes I feel like an anachronism, somebody from the Victorian era when there weren't so many boundaries dividing the sciences.

Vilayanur S. Ramachandran

Novel technologies and ideas that impinge on human biology and their perceived impact on human values have renewed strains in the relationship between science and society.

Paul Berg

Relativity must replace absolutism in the realm of morals as well as in the spheres of physics and biology.

Thomas Cochrane

To address questions of scientific responsibility does not necessarily imply that one needs technical competence in a particular field (e.g. biology) to evaluate certain technical matters.

Serge Lang

As we decipher our biology and learn to modify and adjust it, we are learning to modify ourselves - and we will do so. No laws will stop this.

Gregory Stock

My undergraduate degree was in history, and I wish I had been smart enough to really excel at maths, physics, chemistry or biology because... the voyagers and adventurers and real contributors - that's where they come from.

Michael Moritz

So when I got out of the military, I went back to school in biology, and earned a biology degree at the University of Texas, and then did some graduate work in it.

Elizabeth Moon

The reality of marriage as the union of a mother and a father is grounded in our very biology.

Salvatore J. Cordileone

Fly flight is just a great phenomenon to study. It has everything - from the most sophisticated sensory biology; really, really interesting physics; really interesting muscle physiology; really interesting neural computations.

Michael Dickinson

It's sort of nice in more general terms to see that computational science, computational biology is being recognized. It's become a very large field, and it's always in some ways been the poor sister, or the ugly sister, to experimental biology.

Michael Levitt

Evolution, cell biology, biochemistry, and developmental biology have made extraordinary progress in the last hundred years - much of it since I was weaned on schoolboy biology in the 1930s. Most striking of all is the sudden eruption of molecular biology starting in the 1950s.

John Tyler Bonner

That the role of size has been to some degree neglected in biology may lie in its simplicity. Size may be a property that affects all of life, but it seems pallid compared to the matter which makes up life. Yet size is an aspect of the living that plays a remarkable, overreaching role that affects life's matter in all its aspects.

John Tyler Bonner

One of the major lessons in all of biochemistry, cell biology and molecular medicine is that when proteins operate at the sub cellular level, they behave in a certain way as if they're mechanical machinery.

James Rothman

Game theory is a branch of, originally, applied mathematics, used mostly in economics and political science, a little bit in biology, that gives us a mathematical taxonomy of social life, and it predicts what people are likely to do and believe others will do in cases where everyone's actions affect everyone else.

Colin Camerer

Biology always beats will power.

Mehmet Oz

Through some combination of culture and biology, our minds are intuitively receptive to religion.

Daniel Kahneman

I really wanted to be a doctor, until my freshman year of college when I realized that while I was good at chemistry and biology, I really wasn't feeling challenged by it.

Marissa Mayer

Neuroscience is now a very important research area in biology. We are now understanding a lot more about brains in babies, as well as children and adults.

Robert Winston

The idea would be in my mind - and I know it sounds strange - is that the most important advances in medicine would be made not by new knowledge in molecular biology, because that's exceeding what we can even use. It'll be made by mathematicians, physicists, computer scientists, figuring out a way to get all that information together.

Patrick Soon-Shiong

A National Database on Autism Research is fostering sharing of data and collaborations. Scientists are also making great strides at the interface of biology and engineering with new technologies that are laying the groundwork for future advances.

Thomas R. Insel

I've always been interested in science - one of my favourite books is James Watson's 'Molecular Biology of the Gene.'

Bill Gates

What's been gratifying is to live long enough to see molecular biology and evolutionary biology growing toward each other and uniting in research efforts.

E. O. Wilson

Equity feminism is a moral doctrine about equal treatment that makes no commitments regarding open empirical issues in psychology or biology.

Steven Pinker

For the vast majority of world history, human life - both culture and biology - was shaped by scarcity. Food, clothing, shelter, tools, and pretty much everything else had to be farmed or fabricated, at a very high cost in time and energy.

Martha Beck

Until we recognize the essential role of biology, our attempts to truly unify the universe will remain a train to nowhere.

Robert Lanza

Diminutive worlds are more likely to be rocky, and lapped by oceans and atmospheres. In the vernacular of 'Star Trek,' these would be M-class planets: life-friendly oases where biology could begin and bumpy-faced Klingons might exist.

Seth Shostak

The cosmos is three times as old as Earth. During most of creation's 14 billion year history, our solar system wasn't around. Nonetheless, the early universe still had the right stuff for life, and contained worlds that were just as suitable for spawning biology and intelligence as our own.

Seth Shostak

We haven't yet found a speck of evidence for biology on another world, so we have no objective way to judge whether life is a onetime fluke or a near-inevitable phenomenon.

Seth Shostak

We've accounted for 95 percent of all the stars in the Milky Way. The other 5 percent are big, bright stars - the kind that dominate the night sky, but are lamentably both rare and short-lived. If biology's your thing, you can forget those guys.

Seth Shostak

No, I majored in biology, in a pre-med program.

Neil Diamond

The need to make music, and to listen to it, is universally expressed by human beings. I cannot imagine, even in our most primitive times, the emergence of talented painters to make cave paintings without there having been, near at hand, equally creative people making song. It is, like speech, a dominant aspect of human biology.

Lewis Thomas

I don't believe in technological determinism, especially not in biology and medicine. We have strong laws to keep doctors from monkeying around with humans that will remain in place. It's simply not true that everything that is technologically possible gets done.

Freeman Dyson

Physics investigates the essential nature of the world, and biology describes a local bump. Psychology, human psychology, describes a bump on the bump.

Willard Van Orman Quine

And the actual achievements of biology are explanations in terms of mechanisms founded on physics and chemistry, which is not the same thing as explanations in terms of physics and chemistry.

Michael Polanyi

Wherever there is a design that is highly successful in a broad range of similar environments, it is apt to emerge again and again, independently - the phenomenon known in biology as convergent evolution. I call these designs 'good tricks.'

Daniel Dennett

I have a Ph.D. in cell biology. And that's really manual labor. I mean, experimental science, you do it with your hands. So it's very different. You're out there in a lab, cleaning test tubes, and it just wasn't that fascinating.

Barbara Ehrenreich

The evolution of sex is the hardest problem in evolutionary biology.

John Maynard Smith

The Bible has been through millions of rounds of exegesis and interpretation, but it hasn't been until quite recently that it's been taken as the absolute truth, to the point where people expect it to inform ideas about biology and life on this planet.

Walter Kirn

I think we need to start thinking about grounding our moral systems in our biology.

Frans de Waal

Biology has progressed tremendously due to the model that Darwin put forth. But the black boxes Darwin accepted are now being opened, and our view of the world is again being shaken.

Michael Behe

I was always interested in animals, but when I was little, animal behavior was still a new science. It was available to become a veterinarian, it was available to study biology, but not specifically animal behavior. In the '60s, Jane Goodall was the founder of this new science.

Isabella Rossellini

What an odd time to be a fundamentalist about adaptation and natural selection - when each major subdiscipline of evolutionary biology has been discovering other mechanisms as adjuncts to selection's centrality.

Stephen Jay Gould

I don't believe in any particular definition of the afterlife, but I do believe we're spiritual creatures and more than our biology and that energy cannot be destroyed, but can change. I don't know what the afterlife is going to be, but I'm not afraid of it.

Alan Ball

We have to pay close attention to what we see, and be ready to work with the unexpected according to the basic principles of systems biology and medicine.

Mark Hyman

I entered the literary world, really, from outside. My entire background has been in sciences; I was a biology major in college, then went to medical school. I've never had any formal training in writing.

Khaled Hosseini

Much of modern molecular biology and microbiology has been based on the effort to decipher the basic code of life, which is made up of four nucleotides: adenine, thymine, cytosine, and guanine.

Michael Specter

Culture is how biology responds and makes its living conditions better.

C. J. Cherryh

We were making the first step out of the age of chemistry and physics, and into the age of biology.

Jeremy Rifkin

I loved the idea that biology was logical.

Cynthia Kenyon

Both individual fulfillment and the ecological balance of life on this planet are best served by dying when our inherent biology decrees that we do.

Sherwin B. Nuland

The language of chemistry simply does not mesh with that of biology. Chemistry is about substances and how they react, whereas biology appeals to concepts such as information and organisation. Informational narratives permeate biology.

Paul Davies

At the time I finished high school, I was determined to study biology, deeply convinced to eventually be a researcher.

Christiane Nusslein-Volhard

The major thing is to view biology as an information science.

Leroy Hood

I think people who have all kinds of debilitating mobility issues will benefit from robotic augmentation. That is, even before we get into organ replacement and organ printing and synthetic biology and so on and so forth.

Jason Silva

Tell people that biology and the environment cause obesity and they are offered the one thing we have to avoid: an excuse. As it is, people who see more fat people around them may themselves be more likely to gain weight.

Andrew Lansley

I like problems at the borders of disciplines. One of the reasons that neurobiology of learning and memory appeal to me so much was that I liked the idea of bringing biology and psychology together.

Eric Kandel

I've been around a long time, and I've been interested in memory for a long time. And one of my earlier interests in molecular biology of memory led me to define the switch that converts short term to long term memory.

Eric Kandel

Biology will relate every human gene to the genes of other animals and bacteria, to this great chain of being.

Walter Gilbert

Politics is applied biology.

Ernst Haeckel

Growing up human is uniquely a matter of social relations rather than biology. What we learn from connections within the family takes the place of instincts that program the behavior of animals; which raises the question, how good are these connections?

Elizabeth Janeway

I wanted to be a marine biologist my whole life until I graduated high school. And even now, I'm still like, 'Maybe I'll just quit the biz and go to Santa Cruz and study marine biology and have my own research center in the Bahamas.' Yeah, I'm sure it would be just that smooth.

Cobie Smulders

But while doing that I'd been following a variety of fields in science and technology, including the work in molecular biology, genetic engineering, and so forth.

K. Eric Drexler

Our increasing ability to alter our biology and open up the processes of life is now fueling a new cultural war.

Gregory Stock

It's terrifying the way molecular biology has become more and more jargon ridden. But I strongly believe that my book can be read by the intelligent layman. I want everyone who bought a copy of 'A Brief History of Time' to buy a copy of 'Genome'.

Matt Ridley

The moment I saw the model and heard about the complementing base pairs I realized that it was the key to understanding all the problems in biology we had found intractable - it was the birth of molecular biology.

Sydney Brenner

My boarding school experience was the only thing I had strong enough feelings to write about for hundreds and hundreds of pages. I can still smell the formaldehyde of the fetal pigs in biology.

Curtis Sittenfeld

The subject I was best at in school was biology.

Astrid Berges-Frisbey

If you look at the ecological circuitry of this planet, the ways in which materials like carbon or sulfur or phosphorous or nitrogen get cycled in ways that makes them available for our biology, the organisms that do the heavy lifting are bacteria.

Andrew H. Knoll

As a general rule, biology tends to be conservative. It's rare that evolution 'invents' the same process several times.

Gero Miesenbock

If I could be involved in the hunting and fishing industry, that would be amazing. That said, I studied biology in college and that led into me being really involved in anatomy and being a pre-med major.

Dustin Lynch

One of the central mysteries of biology is why the genome is largely identical from cell to cell, even though cells do different things.

Erez Lieberman Aiden

I started taking a basic biology course, and I really loved it. I started asking research questions incessantly. I was drawn very quickly to biology.

James Rothman

By then, I was making the slow transition from classical biochemistry to molecular biology and becoming increasingly preoccupied with how genes act and how proteins are made.

Paul Berg

I learned about HeLa cells in my first basic biology class, and I just became completely obsessed with them from that point on.

Rebecca Skloot

When I was at school studying biology, I wanted to be a medical researcher. I did work experience at St Mary's Hospital in London, and I begged them to let me see the post mortems. So the first time I saw a naked male was at 15, when I saw an 89 year old man who had died of a brain hemorrhage.

Katherine Parkinson

We have to accept that we are just machines. That's certainly what modern molecular biology says about us.

Rodney Brooks

As physics students, we are taught that physicists are smart, that chemists are moderately acceptable, and that biologists are certainly not very intelligent. So I wasn't inclined to take a biology course. But my father insisted, and maybe what he had in mind was that, if there were no jobs in physics, I would end up being a doctor.

James Rothman

I think that in the 21st century, medical biology will advance at a more rapid pace than before.

Shinya Yamanaka

I was lined up to do this honors degree course in biology, of all things, for no better reason than I got high marks in it. I decided I didn't want to be removing worms' hearts for the rest of my life in Northern Ontario. I thought I would try acting. So, I went to England to study drama. I got Shakespeared out.

Matt Frewer

Becoming a bird ecologist was just luck! I had the chance to be a field assistant for a scientist working in the Galapagos Islands, and while I was there, I saw a particular problem in behavioral biology that I wanted to solve and, in the process, made myself into a bird ecologist.

David J. Anderson

My interest in biology was pretty much always on the philosophical side.

Richard Dawkins

Many differences are rooted in biology and reinforced through culture, so it's important to acknowledge that. Because if you say men and women are the same and if male behaviour is the norm, and women are always expected to act like men, we will never be as good at being men as men are.

Dee Dee Myers

I'm enjoying my life, post-menopause, so much. It's just so great to grow into yourself, and not be bothered with all that tyranny of biology.

Roseanne Barr

A century ago, scientists believed there was only one obvious stomping ground for alien biology in our solar system: Mars. Because it was reminiscent of Earth, Mars was assumed to be chock-a-block with animate beings, and its putative inhabitants got a lot of column inches and screen time.

Seth Shostak

The difference between microeconomics and macroeconomics is a bit like the difference between biology and medicine. Knowing that certain genes increase the risk of cancer is relatively easy. Figuring out exactly which people will get sick, or how to cure them, is a lot more complicated.

Alex Berenson

I went into science, ending up with a Ph.D. in cell biology, but along the way I found out that experimental science involves many hours and days and nights of laboratory work, which is a lot like washing dishes, only a little more challenging. I was too impatient, and maybe a little too sloppy, for it.

Barbara Ehrenreich

Well, biology today as I see it has an amiable look - quite different from the 19th-century view that the whole arrangement of nature is hostile, 'red in tooth and claw.' That came about because people misread Darwin's 'survival of the fittest.'

Lewis Thomas

There's a long tradition in Western thought that humans are not shackled by biology, whereas animals are pure instinct machines.

Frans de Waal

After an extensive interview he arranged for my weaknesses in foreign languages to be over-looked and so I started a Biology degree at Birmingham in 1967.

Paul Nurse

I've always been interested in animal behavior, and I keep reading about it because it's so surprising all the time - so many things are happening around us that we neglect to look at. Part of the passion I have for biology is based on this wonderment.

Isabella Rossellini

One of the great issues in biology is the origin of altruism - of why you would do something for someone else that could hurt you - and Darwin posited that it might be rooted in maternal instinct, in sacrificing yourself for your children.

Isabella Rossellini

I want to know where joy lives. I'd interview scientists, religious leaders and heads of state. I'd want to find out exactly what makes people happy. I'd want to look into the biology, the chemistry of the human brain.

Goldie Hawn

Honestly, I didn't have the patience for biology or history in an academic sense, but I always liked the kind of big questions.

Andrew Bird

But honestly, if you do a rigorous survey of my work, I'll bet you'll find that biology is a theme far more often than physical science.

David Brin

I had gone to school to study marine biology.

Skeet Ulrich

I like writing about biology, not doing it.

Kary Mullis

I'm an amateur science enthusiast. I'm not even a professional enthusiast. I don't know anything; I never even passed biology in high school. But I read the science section of the newspaper.

Dave Eggers

I think it is fine to have sports divided into men's and women's, just as it is fine to say a fifteen-year-old is incapable of consenting to sex. But we should recognize these are social distinctions based on biology, and not categories foisted upon us by nature.

Alice Dreger

The Department of Cell Biology at Johns Hopkins was founded and directed by Tom Pollard, an engaging young scientist with remarkable energy and enthusiasm.

Peter Agre

Biology sets the context, and that is critical, but obesity still boils down to whether a person eats too much or exercises enough.

Robin Marantz Henig

The systems approach to biology will be the dominant theme in medicine.

Leroy Hood

One of my degrees was a science degree in biology.

Elizabeth Moon

I can actually trace the moment I decided I couldn't be a doctor. It was in biology, they brought in these African crickets and we were supposed to dissect them - but there's no way I was touching those bugs.

Meg Rosoff

One of the ultimate challenges of biology is to understand how the brain becomes consciously aware of perception, experience and emotion. But it is equally conceivable that the exchange would be useful for the beholders of art, for people who enjoy art, for historians, and for the artists themselves.

Eric Kandel

There was little in my early life to indicate that an interest in biology would become the passion of my academic career. In fact, there was little to suggest I would have an academic career.

Eric Kandel

I believe God controls the universe. I don't believe biology works in an uncontrolled fashion.

Richard Mourdock

I'd always enjoyed acting at high school, and I was all lined up to do an honours degree course in biology at a Canadian university, and at the eleventh hour the drama teacher I had said, 'You know, you'll get a lot more girls if you go into acting,' and that kinda sold it.

Matt Frewer

Until 1985, when my lab found the protein they are made of, aquaporins hadn't yet been identified. There had been a controversy in biology for more than 100 years about how water moved through cells.

Peter Agre

My work more than didn't fit in. It crossed willy-nilly the boundaries that people had spent their lives building up. It hits some 30 subfields of biology, even geology.

Lynn Margulis

The sweetest thing I could say about my mother and father is that if I had the choice, I would have picked them. But I don't have any belief in biology or DNA as compelling conduct. The idea that we owe people something because we're related to them is bizarre. But the idea that we owe something because of their conduct towards us is legitimate.

Andrew Vachss

Consciousness, for me, is a manifestation of complexity in biology. It's an emergent property.

Gregory Stock

In the late 1970s, when I was a professor at Caltech, I pioneered four instruments for analyzing genes and proteins that revolutionized modern biology - and one of these, the automated DNA sequencer, enabled the Human Genome Project.

Leroy Hood

Most of the people who claim to be doing systems biology are really studying simple and complex molecular machines and how they function, and that is an aspect of systems biology; but it isn't. It's the networks that really capture and store and transmit and integrate and modulate and finally end up executing the biological information as it is.

Leroy Hood

Influenced by him, and probably even more so by my brother Theodore (a year older than me), I soon became interested in biology and developed a respect for the importance of science and the scientific method.

Frederick Sanger

A key issue in developmental biology at that time was the problem of how cells underwent differentiation, with most workers concentrating on explanations in terms of changes in enzyme and gene regulation.

Paul Nurse

I decided that the University of Sussex in Brighton was a good place for this work because it had a strong tradition in bacterial molecular genetics and an excellent reputation in biology.

Paul Nurse

I originally envisioned myself doing something with the suffix 'ology' at the end of it, like marine biology or entomology. But after I started to do some acting gigs, I thought it wasn't a bad thing... I said to myself, 'I might as well keep riding this bus until the wheels fall off.'

Callan McAuliffe

In the present epoch of struggle between two worlds the two opposing and antagonistic trends penetrating the foundations of nearly all branches of biology are particularly sharply defined.

Trofim Lysenko

I was a close observer of the developments in molecular biology.

John Pople

In essence, the science of agronomy is inseparable from biology.

Trofim Lysenko

Usually that's going into biology in a certain way. There's certain strengths and weaknesses to both of the sexes. And I'm not against employing those nor am I against denying those, what I am looking for is a very large array of options.

Mark Morris

I remember being in strong physics, physiology and biology classes.

Barbara Block

Molecular biology has routinely taken problematic things under its wing without altering core ideas.

Ian Hacking

The biggest development in reproductive biology is the birth-control pill. Nobody ever talks about it, but look at the consequences: demographics; aging populations; the sinking population of Europe, Japan; immigration. It's incredible.

Gregory Stock

With my biology degree, I got this job at an environmental lab. We tested sewage runoff, we tested chemical warfare waste runoff. It's a job I'll never do again and I would never wish upon anybody.

Dustin Lynch

I've always liked all the sciences, like math, physics and biology.

Sigrid Agren

And the more profoundly the science of biology reveals the laws of the life and development of living bodies, the more effective is the science of agronomy.

Trofim Lysenko

Even when Darwin's teaching first made its appearance, it became clear at once that its scientific, materialist core, its teaching concerning the evolution of living nature, was antagonistic to the idealism that reigned in biology.

Trofim Lysenko

We know from biology that new forms of organisms simulate their primitive form as closely as possible at first, even though obliged to exist under changed internal and external conditions.

Wilhelm Ostwald

Industrial opportunities are going to stem more from the biological sciences than from chemistry and physics. I see biology as being the greatest area of scientific breakthroughs in the next generation.

George E. Brown, Jr.

In my lab, we're interested in the transition from chemistry to early biology on the early earth.

Jack W. Szostak

As in all of biology, comparative studies showing differences among species are often helpful for a better understanding of the basic mechanisms; with all its advantages, there is a danger of clinging exclusively to one model organism.

John Tyler Bonner

I like to surf. I like to play guitar. I want to do college classes online. I wanted to do marine biology for a long time, but I don't know.

Ali Lohan

I was drawn to biology and history and, of course, art. And I loved languages. The biggest problem I had is that I wasn't taught about the connections between all these things. I think that would have given life a lot more meaning and it would be a lot more enjoyable.

Hussein Chalayan

Biology has tended to be an observational science, and deriving things from first principles has not been possible in the past, but I hate to predict the future on that.

Jeremiah P. Ostriker

Nature is full of drama. I know nothing about biology, about birds, about insects, about the details of politics. I just make movies about human interest stories.

Jacques Perrin

This page is intentionally left blank

This page is intentionally left blank

This page is intentionally left blank

This page is intentionally left blank

This page is intentionally left blank

www.ingramcontent.com/pod-product-compliance
Lightning Source LLC
Chambersburg PA
CBHW071124280526
45787CB00003B/1162